The Ultimate Book of Inspiring Quotes for Young Athletes

Michael Stutman and Kevin Conklin

ISBN: 1540359484
ISBN 13: 978-1540359483

For our children—Ryan, Anna, Daniel, Sean, Jason, Andrew, and Lily—who inspired the InspireMyKids journey and make it real for us every day.

For our wives, Karen and Emily, who lovingly remind us to live these virtues every day and have supported our journeys from day one.

For our parents—Bill, Nancy, Walter, and Joan—who taught us the importance of these values and gave us solid foundations to build from.

For our mentors—Chris, Sharol, and Haylie—for helping to light the spark and continuing to fuel it with their encouragement and feedback.

For the authors of the quotes in this book, for sharing their immense wisdom with the world.

For all the coaches that have taught us and our children not only the fundamentals of sports but the many life lessons that athletics has to offer.

We thank you all from the bottoms of our hearts.

Mike and Kevin

WELCOME

...and thank you for reading InspireMyKids.com's compilation of inspiring quotes for young athletes! Our unwavering goal at InspireMyKids (IMK) is to share inspiring, age-appropriate, real-life stories, pertinent quotes and projects to help children make the world a better place and become the best people they can be.

We've focused this collection on athletics and topics that matter to young athletes' development, not just in sports but also in life. Our editors selected each quote for its potential appeal to children and then validated them based on feedback by children.

Whether you're a child athlete, parent, coach, teacher or mentor, we hope you'll find inspiration in these pages.

To stay abreast of the new quotes we compile and to receive regular updates on real-life, inspiring stories and projects for kids, please visit www. inspiremykids.com to sign up for our email newsletter which we send out no more than once per week. And make sure to check our homepage and quotation page regularly to see what's new!

We welcome and truly encourage your feedback. Please feel free to send a note to info@inspiremykids. com. We hope you find inspiration in these pages, and we hope you'll join us on the IMK journey.

Mike Stutman and the Kevin Conklin

Co-founders, Dads and Coaches
www.inspiremykids.com
mike@inspiremykids.com

INTRODUCTION

There are so many great lessons to learn about life from playing sports. Young people can develop perseverance, teamwork, sportsmanship and many other important character traits through sports. Honing these habits early on can set a young person on the right path in both sports and in life.

This book is a compilation of quotations not only from athletes but great people in history. It is meant to inspire not only athletic achievement but character, as well.

Whether in sports or in life, quotations can provide guidance and wisdom in those critical moments when self-doubt creeps in, when motivation is lacking or when a big decision looms.

We hope you find inspiration in these words to not only be a better athlete but a better person. And if you enjoy what you read here, we encourage you to visit our website, www.inspiremykids.com, for many more quotes and inspirational stories for young people.

TABLE OF CONTENTS

InspireMyKids.com

EFFORT

There are plenty of young athletes who have great talent but lack the drive to give his or her maximum effort to improve. One example of a player who combines talent and hard work is professional basketball's Steph Curry. What separates him from other talented players is his legendary work ethic and ability to give full effort in practice and games.

Always try to do more than what's expected of you and more than you think you can, and good things will happen. Read the quotes below, and you'll notice that many are from the highest achievers in their sport. This is no accident; it's the result not only of their talent but their effort also.

"We all have dreams. But in order to make dreams come into reality, it takes an awful lot of determination, dedication, self-discipline and effort."

– Jesse Owens, Olympic gold medalist, 1936

"If you want to find the real competition, just look in the mirror. After awhile you'll see your rivals scrambling for second place."

– Criss Jami, philosopher and musician

"The Six W's: Work will win, when wishing won't."

– Todd Blackledge, American football player and teacher

"If you train hard, you'll not only be hard, you'll be hard to beat."

– Herschel Walker, pro football player

"Effort only fully releases its reward after a person refuses to quit."

– Napoleon Hill, motivational speaker and author

"There may be people that have more talent than you, but there's no excuse for anyone to work harder than you do."

— Derek Jeter, pro baseball player

"A little more persistence, a little more effort, and what seemed hopeless failure may turn to glorious success."

— Elbert Hubbard, writer and artist, founder of the Roycrofters

"Gold medals are made out of your sweat, blood and tears, and effort in the gym every day, and sacrificing a lot."

— Gabby Douglas, Olympic gold medalist

"Success is peace of mind, which is a direct result of self-satisfaction in knowing you made the effort to become the best of which you are capable."

— John Wooden, college basketball coach

"Much effort, much prosperity."

— Euripides, ancient Greek poet

"Don't measure yourself by what you have accomplished but by what you should have accomplished with your ability."

— John Wooden, college basketball coach

InspireMyKids.com

"The healthiest competition occurs when average people win by putting above average effort."

— Colin Powell, four-star general and former US Secretary of State

"Endless effort, endless humility, endless modesty."

— Rain, South Korean musician and dancer

"Continuous effort—not strength or intelligence—is the key to unlocking our potential."

— Winston Churchill, WWII British prime minister

"Your first projects aren't the greatest things in the world, and they may have no money value, they may go nowhere, but that is how you learn—you put so much effort into making something right if it is for yourself."

— Steve Wozniak, co-founder of Apple

"If things don't come easy, there is no premium on effort. There should be joy in the chase, zest in the pursuit."

— Branch Rickey, baseball player and manager; integrated pro baseball

"Even if you're on the right track, you'll get run over if you just sit there."

— Will Rogers, humorist and author

"Make each day count by setting specific goals to succeed, then putting forth every effort to exceed your own expectations."

– Les Brown, motivational writer and speaker

"Happiness lies in the joy of achievement and the thrill of creative effort."

– Franklin D. Roosevelt, 32nd US President

"The harder you work, the harder it is to surrender."

– Vince Lombardi, pro football coach

"Satisfaction lies in the effort, not in the attainment, full effort is full victory."

– Mahatma Gandhi, leader of the Indian independence movement

"Effort without talent is a depressing situation... but talent without effort is a tragedy.

– Mike Ditka, football player and coach

"An excuse becomes an obstacle in your journey to success when it is made in place of your best effort or when it is used as the object of the blame."

– Bo Bennett, businessman and author

"I've always made a total effort, even when the odds seemed entirely against me. I never quit trying; I never felt that I didn't have a chance to win."

— Arnold Palmer, pro golfer

"You find that you have peace of mind and can enjoy yourself, get more sleep, and rest when you know that it was a one hundred percent effort that you gave— win or lose."

— Gordie Howe, pro hockey player

"Leaders are made, they are not born. They are made by hard effort, which is the price which all of us must pay to achieve any goal that is worthwhile."

— Vince Lombardi, pro football coach

"The road to Easy Street goes through the sewer."

— John Madden, pro football coach and sports broadcasting

"Sweat is the cologne of accomplishment."

— Heywood Hale Broun, sportswriter

"Good, better, best. Never let it rest. Until your good is better and your better is best."

— Tim Duncan, pro basketball player and philanthropist

ATTITUDE

Charles Swindoll once said, "I am convinced that life is 10 percent what actually happens and 90 percent how I react to it." Attitude will shape who you are inside. Are you a glass half full or a glass half empty kind of person? The choice will always be yours.

In sports and in life, adversity will test your attitude. How you respond makes all the difference.

InspireMyKids.com

Like effort, attitude is something you have in your power to control. No matter what your athletic talent is, focus on your effort and your attitude. Your coaches and your teammates will take note.

As John Wooden, the legendary college basketball coach once said, "Things turn out best for the people who make the best of the way things turn out."

Here are some great quotes on attitude.

"Perfection is not attainable, but if we chase perfection we can catch excellence."

– Vince Lombardi, pro football coach

"Attitude is a little thing that makes a big difference."

– Winston Churchill, WWII British prime minister

"Nobody can make you feel inferior without your consent."

– Eleanor Roosevelt, First Lady 1933-1945, humanitarian

"If somebody says no to you, or if you get cut, Michael Jordan was cut his first year, but he came back and he was the best ever. That is what you have to have. The attitude that I'm going to show everybody, I'm going to work hard to get better and better."

– Magic Johnson, pro basketball player

"Nothing can stop the man with the right mental attitude from achieving his goal; nothing on earth can help the man with the wrong mental attitude."

– Thomas Jefferson, Founding Father, Third US President

"Our lives are not determined by what happens to us but how we react to what happens, not by what life brings us but the attitude we bring to life."

– Wade Boggs, pro baseball player

"Coaches will eventually notice a great attitude, and they respect that."

– Heather O'Reilly, pro soccer player

"Ability is what you're capable of doing. Motivation determines what you do. Attitude determines how well you do it."

– Lou Holtz, pro football coach and motivational author

"Let me never fall into the vulgar mistake of dreaming that I am persecuted whenever I am contradicted."

– Ralph Waldo Emerson, essayist and poet

"Things turn out best for the people who make the best of the way things turn out."

– John Wooden, college basketball coach

"My attitude is that if you push me towards something that you think is a weakness, then I will turn that perceived weakness into a strength."

– Michael Jordan, pro basketball player and team owner

"Your attitude, not your aptitude, will determine your altitude."

– Zig Ziglar, motivational speaker and author

"A positive attitude causes a chain reaction of positive thoughts, events and outcomes. It is a catalyst and it sparks extraordinary results."

– Wade Boggs, pro baseball player

"If you are going to achieve excellence in big things, you develop the habit in little matters. Excellence is not an exception, it is a prevailing attitude."

– Colin Powell, four-star general and former US Secretary of State

"I will keep smiling, be positive and never give up! I will give 100 percent each time I play. These are always my goals and my attitude."

– Yani Tseng, pro golfer

"If you don't like something, change it. If you can't change it, change your attitude."

— Maya Angelou, poet and author

"A lot of times I find that people who are blessed with the most talent don't ever develop that attitude, and the ones who aren't blessed in that way are the most competitive and have the biggest heart."

— Tom Brady, pro football player

COURAGE

Courage is the ability to do something that frightens you or to have strength when faced with difficulty. Sports helps reveal and hone your courage. Here are a few examples of courage in sports:

- In sports competitions, you may be faced with a pressure situation when you need to perform your best. It's a difficult task to stare pressure in the face and deliver anyway. This is what courage is all about.

- Every athlete who competes in the Paralympics and Special Olympics shows great courage as they participate in their sports despite some sort of disability, such as missing a leg or being paralyzed.

- Courage is not something that is just meant for sports. It means sticking up for what you believe is right not only on the athletic field but in life, as well. There have been many courageous athletes in the past such as boxing's Muhammad Ali, who demonstrated this kind of courage. He lost a number of his prime years of boxing to stand up for what he believed in, which was refusing to go to war in Vietnam.

Being courageous like this is difficult, but it's a key to your success as an athlete and in life. As Walt Disney said, "All our dreams can come true, if we have the courage to pursue them." Check out these quotes from some very courageous people.

"I learned that courage was not the absence of fear, but the triumph over it. The brave man is not he who does not feel afraid, but he who conquers that fear."

– Nelson Mandela, leader of anti-apartheid movement and President of South Africa

"You've got to take the initiative and play your game. In a decisive set, confidence is the difference."

– Chris Evert, pro tennis player

"Courage is what it takes to stand up and speak; courage is also what it takes to sit down and listen."

– Winston Churchill, WWII British prime minister

"He who is not courageous enough to take risks will accomplish nothing in life."

– Muhammad Ali, pro boxing champion

"The greatest test of courage on earth is to bear defeat without losing heart."

– Robert Green Ingersoll, lawyer, Civil War veteran and political leader

"To uncover your true potential you must first find your own limits and then you have to have the courage to blow past them."

– Picabo Street, Olympic gold medalist, pro skier

"Efforts and courage are not enough without purpose and direction."

– John F. Kennedy, 35th US President

"Courage is the ladder on which all the other virtues mount."

– Clare Boothe Luce, playwright, author, Congressional representative

"I think my mother...made it clear that you have to live life by your own terms and you have to not worry about what other people think and you have to have the courage to do the unexpected."

– Caroline Kennedy, public speaker, daughter of John F. Kennedy and Jacqueline Kennedy Onassis

"Either you decide to stay in the shallow end of the pool or you go out in the ocean."

– Christopher Reeve, actor, public speaker for the disabled

"Inaction breeds doubt and fear. Action breeds confidence and courage. If you want to conquer fear, do not sit home and think about it. Go out and get busy."

– Dale Carnegie, public speaker and motivational author

"The only service a friend can really render is to keep up your courage by holding up to you a mirror in which you can see a noble image of yourself."

– George Bernard Shaw, playwright

"Success is never final, failure is never fatal. It's courage that counts."

– John Wooden, college basketball coach

"All our dreams can come true, if we have the courage to pursue them."

– Walt Disney, entertainment mogul

"We must build dikes of courage to hold back the flood of fear."

– Martin Luther King, Jr., Civil Rights leader

"Some people say I have attitude—maybe I do...but I think you have to. You have to believe in yourself when no one else does—that makes you a winner right there."

– Venus Williams, pro tennis player

"Confidence comes not from always being right but from not fearing to be wrong."

– Peter T. McIntyre, architect

FOCUS AND DETERMINATION

It's easy to get distracted or lose focus on accomplishing your goals both athletically and academically. There's no way around the fact that achieving greatness takes focus, dedication and determination.

Some athletes make it look easy on the playing field. Don't fool yourself; they all put in the necessary work and dedication to be successful. They make sacrifices every day to stay focused on their goals.

InspireMyKids.com

How focused are you in reaching your goals? Check out these quotes on focus and determination.

"When someone tells me "no," it doesn't mean I can't do it, it simply means I can't do it with them."

— Karen E. Quinones Miller, writer

"You will face your greatest opposition when you are closest to your biggest miracle."

— Shannon L. Alder, inspiration writer

"A year from now you may wish you had started today."

— Karen Lamb, writer

"People who lack the clarity, courage, or determination to follow their own dreams will often find ways to discourage yours. Live your truth and don't EVER stop!"

— Steve Maraboli, author of Life, the Truth, and Being Free

"If plan A doesn't work, the alphabet has 25 more letters—204 if you're in Japan."

— Claire Cook, author of Seven Year Switch

"Persistence. Perfection. Patience. Power. Prioritize your passion. It keeps you sane."

– Criss Jami, author

"Doing your best at this moment puts you in the best place for the next moment."

– Oprah Winfrey, entertainment mogul

"You can have anything you want if you want it badly enough. You can be anything you want to be, do anything you set out to accomplish if you hold to that desire with singleness of purpose."

– Abraham Lincoln, 16th US President

"F-E-A-R has two meanings: 'Forget Everything And Run' or 'Face Everything And Rise.' The choice is yours."

– Zig Ziglar, writer and motivational speaker

"Determine that the thing can and shall be done and then...find the way."

– Abraham Lincoln, 16th US President

"Don't wait for your ship to come in, swim out to it."

– Cathy Hopkins, writer

"The wishbone will never replace the backbone."

— Will Henry, writer

"There is a thin line between the impossible and the possible—that is determination."

— Ogwo David Emenike, writer and motivational speaker

"A commitment to never getting knocked down is in reality a decision to never stand up."

— Craig D. Lounsbrough, counselor and writer

PERSEVERANCE

Have you ever really worked toward improving some part of your game, whatever sport it may be? Some are willing to put in the hard work to get better while others just hope they get better with age.

Remember, hope is not a strategy. It takes perseverance to get better at whatever you choose to pursue.

Do you remember watching Derek Jeter in his last year with the Yankees? He continued to take more than 100 ground balls a day always working on the fundamentals of fielding a groundball. It could have been easy for him to say, "I've had a great career. I don't need to improve and work anymore." Jeter realized he can ALWAYS improve, and the only way he can do that is through hard work and perseverance.

Check out these quotes on perseverance.

"Great works are performed not by strength but by perseverance."

– Samuel Johnson, essayist

"Energy and persistence conquer all things."

– Benjamin Franklin, Founding Father

"Perseverance is failing 19 times and succeeding the 20th."

– Julie Andrews, actress and singer

"I am building a fire, and every day I train, I add more fuel. At just the right moment, I light the match."

– Mia Hamm, Olympic gold medalist and pro soccer player

"Champions keep playing until they get it right."

– Billie Jean King, pro tennis player

"Perseverance is not a long race; it is many short races one after the other."

– Walter Elliot, Scottish politician

"Perseverance and perspective until victory."

– Lincoln Diaz-Balart, US politician

"No one succeeds without effort…. Those who succeed owe their success to perseverance."

– Ramana Maharshi, Indian philosopher

"Just remember, you can do anything you set your mind to, but it takes action, perseverance, and facing your fears."

– Gillian Anderson, actress

"You aren't going to find anybody that's going to be successful without making a sacrifice and without perseverance."

– Lou Holtz, college football coach and writer

"I ran and ran and ran every day, and I acquired this sense of determination, this sense of spirit that I would never, never give up, no matter what else happened."

– Wilma Rudolph, Olympic gold medalist

"Football is a great deal like life in that it teaches that work, sacrifice, perseverance, competitive drive, selflessness and respect for authority is the price that each and every one of us must pay to achieve any goal that is worthwhile."

– Vince Lombardi, pro football coach

"The three ordinary things that we often don't pay enough attention to, but which I believe are the drivers of all success, are hard work, perseverance, and basic honesty."

– Azim Premji, Indian businessman

"Somewhere behind the athlete you've become and the hours of practice and the coaches who have pushed you is a little girl who fell in love with the game and never looked back.... Play for her."

– Mia Hamm, Olympic gold medalist and pro soccer player

"If you take short cuts, you will get cut short."

– Andrew WH Conklin, student athlete

"You may encounter many defeats, but you must not be defeated. In fact, it may be necessary to encounter the defeats, so you can know who you are, what you can rise from, how you can still come out of it."

– Maya Angelou, poet and author

"Never, never, never give up!"

– Winston S. Churchill, WWII British prime minister

"It always seems impossible until it's done."

– Nelson Mandela, anti-apartheid leader and President of South Africa

"Many of life's failures are people who did not realize how close they were to success when they gave up."

– Thomas A. Edison, scientist and inventor

"Never confuse a single defeat with a final defeat."

– F. Scott Fitzgerald, author

"If you fell down yesterday, stand up today."

– H.G. Wells, author

HANDLING PRESSURE

Have you ever heard, "he/she choked under pressure"? Pressure can be a difficult thing to overcome in the moment when you can influence the game in either a negative or positive direction. You don't want to let your teammates or yourself down.

Some athletes can harness that energy and rise above it while most of us think about all the things that could go wrong. It's important to learn how to stay "in the moment" and think about nothing more than the task at hand.

Sometimes that's easier said than done, but the more you practice it the better you will get. Here are some quotes on dealing with pressure.

"The team that is the most focused and executes the best is the team that wins. That's usually the team that can handle the pressure of the situation."

– Michael Strahan, pro football player

"Get tough: don't work under pressure; work over pressure."

– Brian Celio, author

"This is normal, to have pressure. It's how you respond. Take the pressure, use the pressure, have fun."

– Chan Ho Park, pro baseball player

"When we long for life without difficulties, remind us that oaks grow strong in contrary winds and diamonds are made under pressure."

– Peter Marshall, Protestant minister and chaplain of the US Senate

"Luck? Sure. But only after long practice and only with the ability to think under pressure."

– Babe Didrikson Zaharias, all-around athlete

"Heart in champions has to with the depth of your motivation and how well your mind and body react to pressure—that is, being able to do what you do best under maximum pain and stress."

– Bill Russell, pro basketball player and coach

"' Pressure' is a word that is misused in our vocabulary. When you start thinking of pressure, it's because you've started to think of failure."

– Tommy Lasorda, pro baseball coach

"Success comes as a result of the pressure exerted upon oneself."

– Sunday Adelaja, Evangelical minister

"No matter how good you are at planning, the pressure never goes away. So I don't fight it. I feed off it. I turn pressure into motivation to do my best."

– Benjamin Carson, neurosurgeon and politician

"Never let the fear of striking out get in your way."

— "Babe" Ruth, pro baseball player

"Relax? How can anybody relax and play golf? You have to grip the club, don't you?"

— Ben Hogan, pro golfer

"A crust eaten in peace is better than a banquet partaken in anxiety."

— Aesop, fabulist

"Concentration is a fine antidote to anxiety."

— Jack Nicklaus, pro golfer

"Sports do not build character. They reveal it."

— John Wooden, college basketball coach

"Let pressure pass over and through you. That way you can't be harmed by it."

— Brian Herbert, author

InspireMyKids.com

FACING ADVERSITY

When things are going well and all's right with the world, life can be great. But how do you react when things aren't going well?

It might be easy to give up and get discouraged or blame someone or something else for your situation. This is the time to figure out not only what you can control but how you are going to react to what has happened also.

What can you learn from this experience that will help you in the future? You can always control how you respond to adversity.

Have you ever had a friend, who no matter what happens, stays positive? Can you try that in your life for a day and see what happens?

Here are some inspirational quotes on facing adversity.

"There is no education like adversity."

— Benjamin Disraeli, British politician and prime minister

"Everyone goes through adversity in life, but what matters is how you learn from it."

— Lou Holtz, college football coach and writer

"Every adversity, every failure, every heartache carries with it the seed of an equal or greater benefit."

— Napoleon Hill, author and motivational speaker

"Nearly all men can stand adversity, but if you want to test a man's character, give him power."

— Abraham Lincoln, 16th President of the US

"The eagle has no fear of adversity. We need to be like the eagle and have a fearless spirit of a conqueror!"

– Joyce Meyer, Christian author and speaker

"If you live long enough, you'll make mistakes. But if you learn from them, you'll be a better person. It's how you handle adversity, not how it affects you. The main thing is never quit, never quit, never quit."

– William J. "Bill" Clinton, 42nd President of the US

"If you're doing your best, You will not have the time to worry about Failures and Losses."

– Unknown

"Adversity causes some men to break; others to break records."

– William Arthur Ward, writer

"We don't develop courage by being happy every day. We develop it by surviving difficult times and challenging adversity."

– Barbara de Angelis, psychologist and author

"Show me someone who has done something worthwhile, and I'll show you someone who has overcome adversity."

– Lou Holtz, college football coach and writer

"One thing about championship teams is that they're resilient. No matter what is thrown at them, no matter how deep the hole, they find a way to bounce back and overcome adversity."

– Nick Saban, college football coach

"Just as we develop our physical muscles through overcoming opposition—such as lifting weights— we develop our character muscles by overcoming challenges and adversity."

– Stephen Covey, businessman and author

"Someone said adversity builds character, but someone else said adversity reveals character. I'm pleasantly surprised with my resilience. I persevere, and not just blindly. I take the best, get rid of the rest, and move on, realizing that you can make a choice to take the good."

– Brooke Shields, actress

"Adversity is the state in which man most easily becomes acquainted with himself, being especially free of admirers then."

– John Wooden, college basketball coach

"One thing that I don't think my critics realize about me is that I've been trained to look adversity in the face."

– Reggie White, pro football player

SPORTSMANSHIP

There are many examples of individuals and teams that have shown great teamwork and sportsmanship.

For example, a college girl's softball team once carried an opposing player around the bases after she hit a homerun but injured herself rounding first base and could not walk. Those girls who picked this opposing player up showed tremendous sportsmanship.

Your challenge is to be the person on your team who is remembered for your sportsmanship. By doing so, you will not just be improving yourself and your team but improving the world around you.

Here are some great quotes on sportsmanship.

"I think sportsmanship is knowing that it is a game, that we are only as a good as our opponents, and whether you win or lose, to always give 100 percent."

– Sue Wicks, pro basketball player

"One man practicing sportsmanship is far better than a hundred teaching it."

– Knute Rockne, college football coach

"Golf is a game of respect and sportsmanship; we have to respect its traditions and its rules."

– Jack Nicklaus, pro golfer

"The mark of great sportsmen is not how good they are at their best, but how good they are at their worst."

– Martina Navratilova, pro tennis player

InspireMyKids.com

"After I hit a homerun I had a habit of running the bases with my head down. I figured the pitcher already felt bad enough without me showing him up rounding the bases."

— Mickey Mantle, pro baseball player

"Sportsmanship for me is when a guy walks off the court and you really can't tell whether he won or lost, when he carries himself with pride either way."

— Jim Courier, pro tennis player

"What lies behind us and what lies before us are small matters compared to what lies within us."

— Ralph Waldo Emerson, essayist and author

"Kind words can be short and easy to speak, but their echoes are truly endless."

— Mother Teresa, Roman Catholic nun (now Saint Teresa of Calcutta)

"To succeed . . . you need to find something to hold on to, something to motivate you, something to inspire you."

— Tony Dorsett, pro football player

TEAMWORK

Think about the best team you were ever on. Not just the one that won the most games but the one that worked together the best. What was it like to be on that team?

The best teams trust each other and hold each other accountable for the greater good of the team. They inspire and support each other.

InspireMyKids.com

It's a great thing to work toward a common goal together versus just simply focusing on yourself. And it takes great teammates to be part of a great team. You can choose to be that great teammate.

Here are some inspiring quotes about teamwork.

"Unity is strength.... When there is teamwork and collaboration, wonderful things can be achieved."

– Mattie Stepanek, poet and motivational speaker

"Talent wins games, but teamwork and intelligence win championships."

– Michael Jordan, pro basketball player

"Teamwork is what the Green Bay Packers were all about. They didn't do it for individual glory. They did it because they loved one another."

– Vince Lombardi, pro football coach

"To me, teamwork is the beauty of our sport, where you have five acting as one. You become selfless."

– Mike Krzyzewski, college football coach

"Teamwork is the fuel that allows common people to produce uncommon results."

— Unknown

"The best kids are going to become the best. But the best thing about it is that you're going to learn lessons in playing those sports about winning and losing and teamwork and teammates and arguments and everything else that are going to affect you positively for the rest of your life."

— Carl Lewis, Olympic gold medalist

"Alone we can do so little; together we can do so much."

— Helen Keller, deaf and blind author

"It is amazing how much you can accomplish when it doesn't matter who gets the credit."

— Unknown

"Gettin' good players is easy. Gettin' 'em to play together is the hard part."

— Casey Stengel, pro baseball coach

"We're a team. One person struggles, we all struggle.
One person triumphs, we all triumph."

— Unknown

"Teamwork divides the task and doubles the success."

— Unknown

"A successful team beats with one heart."

— Unknown

InspireMyKids.com

HUMILITY

It's good to be confident in yourself and to always strive to be the best you can be. Yet, truly successful people strive not only to be their best but to be great in how they treat others and celebrate their talents.

For example, you may have seen an athlete who scores a touchdown, drops the ball and goes down on his knees to give thanks for his achievement. Or another player who scores but then runs around the field pointing at himself and calling attention to his or her achievement. One of these people is being humble and grateful, while the other is being arrogant and boastful.

In today's world of professional sports, there seems to be a lot of self-congratulations rather than humility. You don't need to follow that path.

Humility is about being modest, showing respect and putting others before yourself. It isn't calling attention to yourself or being rude. It's about gratitude. It's about good sportsmanship.

Humility is not just for the ball field, it's something to apply to every aspect of your life. The most respected athletes sooner or later realize that having real humility does not take away from their self-worth but adds to it.

It's important to have humility when you play sports and in life. Telling someone how good you are at something is a lot different from just going out and being good.

Eli Manning of the New York Giants epitomizes an athlete with plenty of confidence and talent but also full of humility. He never talks about his own accomplishments but tends to always put talking about the team as a whole first.

Here are some great quotations about humility.

"The proud man counts his newspaper clippings, the humble man his blessings."

— Fulton Sheen, Roman Catholic priest and motivational speaker

"I don't care how old you are, there's a level of humility that comes with that."

— Billy Donovan, pro basketball coach

"In the process of trial and error, our failed attempts are meant to destroy arrogance and provoke humility."

— Master Kwon, martial arts instructor

"Humility is attentive patience."

— Simone Weil, philosopher and political activist

"With pride, there are many curses. With humility, there come many blessings."

— Ezra Taft Benson, Mormon religious leader

"Well done is better than well said."

— Benjamin Franklin, Founding Father

"The really tough thing about humility is you can't brag about it."

— Gene Brown, college basketball player

"True humility is not thinking less of yourself; it's thinking of yourself less."

— C. S. Lewis, author

"Humility is the solid foundation of all virtues."

— Confucius, ancient Chinese philosopher

"I claim to be a simple individual liable to err like any other fellow mortal. I own, however, that I have humility enough in me to confess my errors and to retrace my steps."

— Mahatma Gandhi, Indian civil rights leader

"We come nearest to the great when we are great in humility."

— Rabindranath Tagore, poet and author

"It ain't the heat, it's the humility."

— Yogi Berra, pro baseball player

 InspireMyKids.com

"Humility is the true key to success. Successful people lose their way at times. They often embrace and overindulge from the fruits of success. Humility halts this arrogance and self-indulging trap. Humble people share the credit and wealth, remaining focused and hungry to continue the journey of success."

– Rick Pitino, college basketball coach

LEADERSHIP

Are you a leader of your sports team? Every team needs good leaders. And, certainly, the world needs good leaders! Sports is a great place to develop your leadership skills.

What do leaders do? They are those who step to the front of the line and lead by words and example. They do the right thing without being asked or when no one is watching. They help and guide teammates in need. They set good examples for others and are seen as role models. They stand up for their teammates and what they believe in even when it may be the hard thing to do.

People naturally follow leaders. And while being a leader has a lot of rewards, it has a lot more responsibility.

Mark Messier, a captain for the New York Rangers when they won the Stanley Cup, is one athlete who comes to mind when thinking of a true leader. He not only led by example but also made all his teammates around him better.

Check out these inspiring quotes on being a leader.

"Solve someone's problems and you produce a follower. Teach someone to solve their own problems and you produce a leader."

— Alexander Den Heijer, inspirational speaker

"Leadership is diving for a loose ball, getting the crowd involved, getting other players involved. It's being able to take it as well as dish it out. That's the only way you're going to get respect from the players."

— Larry Bird, pro basketball player

"Leadership is practiced not so much in words as in attitude and in actions."

– Harold S. Geneen, businessman

"If you think you can do a thing or think you can't do a thing, you're right."

– Henry Ford, inventor and founder of Ford Motor Company

"Today a reader, tomorrow a leader."

– Margaret Fuller, journalist

"The cautious seldom err."

– Confucius, ancient Chinese philosopher

"High expectations are the key to everything."

– Sam Walton, businessman and founder of Walmart

"The strength of a team is in making up for each other's weaknesses. United they can attain a goal in time."

– Sunday Adelaja, Evangelical minister

"Hold yourself responsible for a higher standard than anybody expects of you. Never excuse yourself."

– Henry Ward Beecher, Protestant minister and abolitionist

InspireMyKids.com

"A good leader takes a little more than his share of the blame, a little less than his share of the credit."

— Arnold H. Glasow, businessman

"If the highest aim of a captain were to preserve his ship, he would keep it in port forever."

— Thomas Aquinas, Roman Catholic saint

"You don't inspire people by showing how powerful you are. You inspire people by showing how powerful they are."

— Alexander Den Heijer, inspirational speaker

"Being positive in a negative situation is not naive. It's leadership."

— Ralph Marston, football player

"Where there is no vision, there is no hope."

— George Washington Carver, botanist and teacher

CONCLUSION

We at InspireMyKids hope that you enjoyed reading these quotes and that the words inspire you to not only become a better athlete but a better person as well.

We encourage you to pick out your favorite quotes and write them down somewhere where you can look at them regularly as a reminder.

Athletics are a great measuring stick to test yourself in so many different ways. It's easy to try and compare yourself with your friends or teammates. The real challenge is trying to be the best you can be, constantly to improve every day and strive to help your team become its best.

It's amazing what you can accomplish when you constantly strive to get better at whatever you choose to do in life. If you can look at yourself in the mirror and know you tried your best and gave the most to your team, you'll begin to feel very good about yourself, regardless of the outcome.

Always remember to have fun and enjoy yourself. Life is too short to not enjoy what you're doing. This doesn't mean quit at the first sign of adversity. It just means that it's important to appreciate where you are and what you're trying to accomplish.

And don't forget to thank your parents or parent and coaches for supporting you in all your athletic activities. They give so much of their time so that you can reach your full potential as an athlete and person.

Mike Stutman and Kevin Conklin

Dads, Coaches and Co-founders InspireMyKids.com

www.inspiremykids.com

mike@inspiremykids.com

We hope you find this book inspiring and that many of the quotes help inspire your own

journey to become the best version of yourself, both on and off the field.

We also hope this is the beginning, not the end, of our interaction with you. If you like what you found in this book, and you have not already done so, please consider joining InspireMyKids to help children become their best and make the world a better place.

To stay abreast of new quotes that we compile, books we publish, and real-life, inspiring stories and projects for kids, please visit our website- inspiremykids.com—to sign up for our e-mail list and connect with us on social media.

Also, the educator section of our website includes ideas to start incorporating inspirational quotes into your school or class, access to worksheets, common core lesson plans and professional development options for educators.

We truly welcome your feedback.

- What quote topics do you want us to explore next?

- Do you have a favorite quote you would like us to include in our next edition or book?

- What books would you like to see us publish next?

Just drop us a line at info@inspiremykids.com

73179846R00041

Made in the USA
Columbia, SC
02 September 2019